ARIZONA

in words and pictures

BY DENNIS B. FRADIN

ILLUSTRATIONS BY RICHARD WAHL

MAPS BY LEN MEENTS

Consultant
    Mary Choncoff
    Education Program Specialist
    Arizona Department of Education

 CHILDRENS PRESS, CHICAGO

To Elsie

and Harold

Bloom

The Grand Canyon

Library of Congress Cataloging in Publication Data

Fradin, Dennis B.
  Arizona in words and pictures.

  SUMMARY: Presents a brief history and description
of the Grand Canyon State.
  1. Arizona—Juvenile literature. [1. Arizona]
I. Meents, Len W.   II. Wahl, Richard, 1939-
III. Title.
F811.3.F72   979.1   79-21480
ISBN 0-516-03903-2

    3 4 5 6 7 8 9 10 11 12 R 87 86 85 84 83 82 81

Picture Acknowledgments:
ARIZONA OFFICE OF TOURISM: 2, 15, 17 (left), 25, 30, 32, 41
NATIONAL PARK SERVICE PHOTO, RICHARD FREAR: 5, 42 (right)
NATIONAL PARK SERVICE PHOTO BY CECIL W. STOUGHTON,
42 (left)
FLAGSTAFF CHAMBER OF COMMERCE: 6
CHRIS HAGEL: cover, 7, 11, 22, 23, 27, 29, 35 (right), 37, 38
DEPARTMENT OF THE INTERIOR, NATIONAL PARK SERVICE, PHOTO
BY W.E. DUTTON: 16
TUCSON CONVENTION & VISITORS BUREAU: 17 (right), 33, 34,
35 (left)
FMC CORPORATION: 18
NATIONAL PARK SERVICE PHOTO BY FRED MANG, JR.: 26, 40
METEOR CRATER ENTERPRISES, INC.: 28
FISH & WILDLIFE SERVICE: 39
COVER PICTURE: Organ pipe cactus, Papago Park

Arizona

Arizona (air • ah • ZONE • ah) comes from an Indian word, *Arizonac.* It probably means "little spring." Arizona is a big state in southwestern United States. It is famous for breathtaking scenery. Arizona has the Grand Canyon. The Painted Desert glows with lovely colors. Arizona's Petrified (PEH • tra • fied) Forest has trees that have turned to stone.

Do you know where Hopi (HO • pee) Indians live in a village that is 800 years old?

Do you know where the Apache (a • PATCH • ee) chiefs Cochise (ko • CHEESS) and Geronimo fought for their land?

Do you know where the "Gunfight at the O.K. Corral" took place?

As you will learn, the answer to all these questions is—the Grand Canyon State, Arizona.

The first people lived in Arizona over 20,000 years ago. One early group is now called the Basket Makers. They wove baskets and clothes. They raised squash and beans. They often lived in caves.

The Pueblo (PWEB • lo) people came later. They lived in villages, called *pueblos* in Spanish. Some of their houses were made of stone. Others were made of *adobe* (sun-dried bricks made of clay and straw). Their buildings were sometimes four stories high. They made pottery. They grew cotton and made cotton clothes.

The Cliff Dwellers also lived in Arizona. Many lived high up in the mountains. Cliff Dweller ruins can be seen at Tonto National Monument.

Tonto National Monument

Another group is now called the Hohokam (HO • ho • kum) people. They built canals to bring water to their farms. They are also known as the Canal Builders.

Throughout Arizona you can see relics of ancient (AIN • chent) people. They built ball fields. They made jewelry. They made fine tools. These early people are thought to be related to Indians who live in Arizona today.

Hopi Indians still make pottery, baskets, and dolls, called *kachinas*.

The Hopi Indians are related to the Pueblo people of long ago. When Spanish explorers came to Arizona they found the Hopi living in pueblos. They grew corn and beans. Hopi women and girls sang while they ground their corn. They made a thin bread, called *piki*, out of the corn. Hopi Indians made pottery and baskets. They raised sheep and burros. Their rain dance was known as the "Snake Dance." For many years the Hopi Indians were ruled by women.

The Pima Indians lived along the Gila (HEE • la) River. They were known as the "River People." They were peaceful farmers. The Pima Indians are closely related to the Papago (PAH • pa • go) — "Bean People." The Papago Indians are one of the oldest tribes in Arizona. They have been there over 11,000 years. The Pima and Papago Indians used the plants of the desert. They made rope, baskets, sandals, and thread out of the fibers of yucca (YUCK • a) leaves. They ate the fruit of cactus plants.

Yucca plant

Other tribes were more warlike. The Mojave (mo •
HAV • ee) Indians could be very fierce. They fought with
bows and arrows. They farmed. They fished in the
Colorado (kah • low • RAH • do) River.

In their early days, Apache hunters traveled across
the land. They were nomads, which means they didn't
stay in one place for long. "Forgive me for killing you,
little brother," an Apache would ask an animal killed for
food. They believed that the animals' spirits would live
on in the spirit world. Later, the Apache became farmers
and cattlemen. They were noted for their dances and
songs. They worshipped a nature god, known as Usen. At
one time the Apache were the fiercest tribe in the
southwest. Their war chief led them in battle. In times of
peace the Apache, like the Hopi, were ruled by women.

The Navajo (NAV • a • ho) Indians were closely related to the Apache. The Navajo were hunters and farmers, too. They also were nomads. They built earth-covered, wooden huts, called *hogans*. The Navajo Indians learned to raise sheep. They were fine horseback riders. The Navajo are well known for beautiful woven rugs and blankets and silvercraft.

One small, interesting Arizona tribe is the Havasupai (ha • VAH • soo • pi). They were living at the bottom of the Grand Canyon when Spanish explorers arrived.

Spanish explorers were the first white men in Arizona. The Spanish controlled Mexico, south of Arizona. They heard stories about a kingdom in American made of gold. The kingdom was called the Seven Cities of Cibola (SEE • .bow • la). The streets in these cities were said to be made of gold. The walls were made of jewels. One Spanish explorer, Coronado, entered the Arizona and New Mexico area in 1540. He led hundreds of soldiers. He never found the cities of gold. Instead, he found Indian villages. The same year, the Spaniard de Cardenas (day car • DAY • nus) explored the Grand Canyon. The Spanish didn't see any gold there, either. However, Spain did claim the area we now call Arizona.

Years later, Spanish priests came to Arizona. The priests wanted the Indians to give up their own religion. They wanted them to become Christians. Settlements,

San Xavier del Bac Mission

called *missions*, were built. Father Eusebio Kino (u • SEE
• be • o KEY • no) built seven missions in Arizona. The
most famous was San Xavier del Bac (SAN ZAIV • yur
DEL BOK) Mission. The Indians called it the White Dove
of the Desert. It is near Tucson (TWO • sahn).

Spanish soldiers came with the priests. The Indians were forced to work like slaves at the missions. Many Indians fought the Spanish. In 1680 the Hopi Indians killed a number of priests and burned their churches. Apache, Pima (PEE • ma), and Papago Indians fought the Spanish, too. Maricopa (mah • ree • COE • pah) and Yuma (YOU • mah) Indians were friendly to men such as Father Kino. Father Kino showed them how to grow new kinds of vegetables. He helped them raise cattle and sheep.

In 1752 Spanish soldiers built the first *presidio* (pray • SEE • dyo) (fort) in Arizona, at Tubac. In 1776 a fort was built at Tucson. Through the years, Apache and other

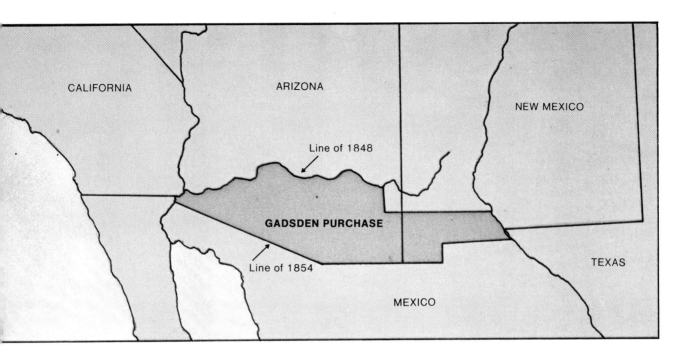

Indians fought the Spanish soldiers who manned these forts. Despite much fighting, the Indians who wanted to drive the Spanish out could not do so.

In 1821 Mexico became independent of Spain. Mexico took control of Arizona. But in 1846 the United States went to war against Mexico. The United States won. The United States took part of Arizona from Mexico in 1848. By the Gadsden (GADS • den) Purchase of 1853, the United States received the rest of Arizona. In 1863 Arizona was made into a territory (TAIR • ah • torry).

The Arizona Territory was a land of gold mines, cowboy towns, shootings, hangings, and Indian wars.

Many of Arizona's first settlers came to look for metals. Some mined silver. Some mined copper. And some mined gold. During the middle of the 1800s Americans had gold fever. Gold had been discovered in California. Many people rushed into the mountains of Arizona looking for gold. A few found rich veins of gold.

The greatest gold find in Arizona was by Henry Wickenburg, in 1864. Wickenburg was looking for gold in the hills of western Arizona. According to the story, Wickenburg's burro left camp. Wickenburg chased it through the hills. He picked up some stones to throw at the stubborn animal. The stones were very heavy. They were solid gold! This was the start of the Vulture (VUL • chur) Mine, Arizona's biggest.

Towns were built where gold and silver were mined. Tombstone, Bisbee, Globe, and Gila City were four mining towns. Mining towns were rough, tough places. Miners sometimes fought each other with guns and fists. Indians attacked miners when they were out in the hills. Gamblers came to mining towns to "strike it rich" at the gambling tables.

Tombstone

A roundup at Pipe Spring.

Sometimes the gold or silver mines gave out. People left the towns. Towns such as Silver King, and Vulture City became "ghost towns" where no one lived.

Many miners who went broke decided to set up ranches and farms. In the 1870s many ranches and farms were started along the Gila River.

Cowboys worked on the ranches. The cowboys took care of the cattle. They branded them. They rounded them up. They built fences. Cowboys did carry guns. Often they were used to protect the cattle from mountain lions and other wild animals. But sometimes cowboys got into gunfights. Cattle "rustlers" stole

A cowboy's life is no longer dangerous, but it can be lonely on the large ranches.

cattle. Then the cowboys would go out with their guns to hunt them down.

After a big roundup, cowboys often went into Benson and other towns for fun. Some might gamble. Before you knew it, fists would be flying and six-shooters blazing. Sometimes, also, cowboys fought lawmen. But the gunfighting was unusual. Mainly, being a cowboy was hard work.

In 1857, stagecoaches began carrying mail and people through Arizona. Indians attacked the stagecoaches. So did gangs of outlaws.

Coal being delivered to a power plant on
Lake Powell.

In 1878 the Southern Pacific Railroad crossed into
Arizona from California. Trains brought more people to
Arizona. Between 1870 and 1880 the number of people in
Arizona grew from about 10,000 to about 40,000.

Through the years, the Indians battled the settlers
who were taking their lands. The Navajo Indians fought.
In 1863 the Indian fighter Kit Carson came to Arizona.
In 1863-1864 Carson and some soldiers captured 7,000
Navajo Indians in Canyon de Chelly. They were taken
out of Arizona and into New Mexico. Later, the Navajo
were allowed to return to Arizona. They have grown into
the largest tribe in the United States.

Many Apache Indians fought. Chief Cochise was a great Apache warrior. In 1862 Cochise led the Apaches in a fight against U.S. soldiers at Apache Pass. For many years Cochise led attacks against stagecoaches, ranches, and towns. Cochise was never beaten. He finally agreed to a peace treaty. There was only one white man Cochise trusted. His name was Tom Jeffords. He owned a stagecoach line. Cochise and Jeffords became good friends. They became blood brothers. In 1872, Jeffords and Cochise finally worked out terms of peace.

COCHISE

Geronimo was one Apache chief who continued to fight. Geronimo was very angry. His wife and children had been murdered. From about 1876 to 1886 Geronimo fought settlers in Mexico, New Mexico, and Arizona. Finally, in 1886 the mighty Geronimo surrendered in Arizona's Skeleton Canyon.

With the capture of Geronimo, Indian wars ended in Arizona. Now that Arizona was safe from attacks by Indians and bandits, more and more settlers came.

During the 1890s many people wanted Arizona to become a state. Finally, on February 14, 1912, Arizona became our 48th state.

The first governor of the new state was George W. P. Hunt. He served seven terms. He worked on laws to help the miners and ranchers. He worked on laws to create dams. A number of dams—such as Roosevelt Dam, Coolidge Dam, and Hoover Dam—were built in Arizona over the years. The dams store water that can be used on farms when it is needed. Bringing water from one place to another is called *irrigation*. If not for irrigation, much Arizona farmland would still be desert.

Farmers grew crops of cotton, fruits, and vegetables. Others had cattle ranches. More people came to Arizona to farm and ranch, towns and cities grew.

Oak Creek
Canyon

People came to Arizona because of the sunshine. Many
chose Phoenix (FEE • nix) as their retirement home.
Many people went to Arizona for vacations. So Arizona
became a state where tourists spend a lot of money.

The clear Arizona skies attracted many other people.
Air Force bases were set up in Arizona during World
War II (1939-1945). With all those sunny days, Arizona
was a good place for pilots to practice.

But the people who had been there first — the Indians
— weren't doing so well. Most Indians lived on land kept
especially for them — called *reservations*. During World

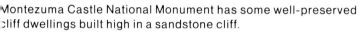
Montezuma Castle National Monument has some well-preserved
cliff dwellings built high in a sandstone cliff.

War II, the Navajo Indians helped their country in an unusual way. The Navajo language is very complex. The United States Army used it to send messages in code. No enemy spies could figure out those messages. Despite helping their country in the war, it took until 1948 for Indians to get the right to vote in Arizona. Many Indians worked hard to improve life for themselves. The Navajo Indians found coal, oil, and uranium on their land. These helped them make money. They also started motels and other businesses. In 1969 Navajo Community College was built on the Navajo reservation.

You have read about some of Arizona's history. Now it is time to take a trip—in words and pictures—through the Grand Canyon State.

Most of northern Arizona is called the Plateau (plah • TOE) Region. It has a lot of high, flat land gouged out by canyons. The Grand Canyon is in the Plateau Region. So is Arizona's highest mountain—Humphreys (HUM • freez) Peak. Humphreys Peak is 12,633 feet above sea level. The Plateau Region has deserts, such as the Painted Desert. And it has forests.

The southern part of Arizona (plus part of the northwest) is called the Basin and Range Region. It has more mountain ranges than the Plateau Region. These mountains have heavy forests. It has big valleys, good for growing crops. And it has a lot of low-lying, flat desert land. The biggest cities in Arizona—Phoenix and Tucson—are in this region.

The Grand Canyon

The Grand Canyon is a good place to begin your trip
through Arizona. It is in Grand Canyon National Park in
northwest Arizona. Many call the Grand Canyon the
most beautiful place in this beautiful state. Some call it
the most amazing natural wonder of the *world*. The
waters of the Colorado River flow at the bottom on the
canyon. The canyon is over a mile deep in places. It is up
to 18 miles wide. The Canyon is colorful, old, and big.

The Grand Canyon was formed by water. The waters of the Colorado River helped carve out the Grand Canyon. This took millions of years.

There are ruins of Indian villages in the area that are almost a thousand years old. A number of Indian tribes—including the Hopi, Navajo, and Havasupai—still live in the area of the Grand Canyon. The Havasupai is the little tribe that lives at the bottom of the Grand Canyon.

Grand Canyon is not the only canyon in Arizona. Oak Creek Canyon, Marble Canyon, Canyon de Chelly, and Monument Canyon are some others. Footprints of dinosaurs can be seen at Dinosaur Canyon, which is about 60 miles north of Flagstaff.

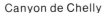
Canyon de Chelly

The Painted Desert (above) and the
Petrified Forest (right)

The Painted Desert is east of the Grand Canyon. It
lies along the Little Colorado River. Few plants live
here. It has bright-colored sand, rocks, and clay. You can
see blue, pink, yellow, brown, and blood-red sands and
rocks there. Because of the dust from the desert, even
the air sometimes glows with a pink-purple haze. The
Navaho Indians use the sands from the Painted Desert to
make sand paintings.

Petrified Forest National Park is southeast of the
Painted Desert. Once this was a forest of live trees. The
trees got old and fell. Rivers flooded in the area. They
brought in sand to cover the trees. Minerals seeped into
the wood. The minerals turned the wood to stone.

Meteor
Crater

One of the greatest natural wonders in Arizona was made by a visitor from space. About half way between the Grand Canyon and the Petrified Forest is a very unusual hole in the ground. This hole is almost a mile wide. It is 600 feet deep. It is thought to have been made by a huge meteor that collided with the earth. Most meteors (called "shooting stars") are no bigger than pebbles. Only very rarely does a huge meteor collide with Earth. The meteor itself has never been found.

Flagstaff is the biggest city in northern Arizona. Lumbering is done in the nearby forests. Lowell Observatory is at Flagstaff. A large telescope is there. Dr. Percival Lowell built it in 1894. He used it to study

Ruins at Casa Grande National Monument.

the planet Mars. In 1930, a very important discovery
was made at Lowell Observatory. This was the planet
Pluto. It appeared as a speck of light on a photo. Clyde
W. Tombaugh (TOM • boh) found Pluto.

Arizona's biggest cities are in the southern part of the
state.

Phoenix is the biggest city. Over 700,000 people live in
Phoenix. It is the capital of Arizona.

Hundreds of years ago, the Hohokam Indians lived in
this area. They built canals to bring water to their crops.
They lived here until about 1400. At Casa Grande
National Monument, southeast of Phoenix, you can see

Phoenix

remains of their villages and canals. At Pueblo Grande,
in Phoenix, canals and adobe houses have been found.

Phoenix was settled by 1868. Miners came to the area.
Ranchers came. And farmers came.

Phoenix was named for a mythical bird. The ancient
Egyptians (e • JIP • shunz) said that the phoenix lived to
be 500 years old. Then it died in a fire. But the bird rose
again out of its own ashes. The city was given this name
because the settlers thought that a new city would grow
up on the ancient city of the Hohokams.

Today, water must still be brought to the Phoenix area for the crops. The water is stored behind dams, such as Roosevelt Dam. Cotton, fruits, and vegetables are grown.

The fruits and vegetables are packed in Phoenix. Then they are sent to other places in Arizona and the rest of the United States. Chemicals and computers are made in Phoenix. Meat is packed here, too.

The Arizona State Capitol Building

Visit the Arizona State Capitol Building in Phoenix.
This is where Arizona lawmakers meet. There are many
gardens on the capitol grounds. One garden has different
kinds of cactus plants that grow in Arizona. If the
lawmakers are meeting, you can watch them.

Visit Papago Park. The Desert Botanical Garden is
there. It has a collection of cactus plants and other desert
plants. The Phoenix Zoo is also in Papago Park.

At the Heard Museum you can learn about the Indians.
And at the Pioneer Living History Museum you can
learn about Arizona's pioneer days.

Mesa (MAY • sah) is Arizona's third biggest city. The Mormons, a religious group, founded Mesa in 1878. Sugar beets, melons, and lettuce are grown in Mesa. Then they are packed and sent to other places.

Tempe is Arizona's fourth biggest city. It is the home of Arizona State University.

Scottsdale is the fifth biggest city in Arizona. People like to vacation there.

Glendale has the Luke Air Force Base nearby. Boxes, machinery, and bicycle parts are made in Glendale. Many kinds of fruits and vegetables are shipped from Glendale to the rest of the United States.

Tucson is 121 miles southeast of Phoenix. Tucson is Arizona's second biggest city.

Old Tucson

Missiles and electrical machinery are made in the city. Because of its dry desert air and sunshine, many people go to Tucson for the winter. A lot of people like to see a rodeo that is held in Tucson every February.

Tucson is the home of the University of Arizona. Visit the Arizona State Museum at the university. You can see relics of Indians who lived over 10,000 years ago.

Visit Old Tucson in Tucson Mountain Park. Here a village has been built to show how Tucson looked a hundred years ago. Many Western movies and TV shows have been shot here.

The Tucson rodeo

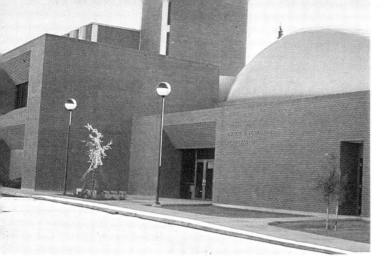

The University of Arizona   The O.K. Corral in Tombstone

There are interesting small towns to visit in southern Arizona. Visit Globe. It got its name from a globe-shaped boulder made of silver. In the 1870s Globe was packed with silver miners.

Visit Tombstone, in southeast Arizona. It was once a mining and cowboy town. It became known as "The Town Too Tough to Die."

The most famous gunfight at Tombstone was in 1881, at the O.K. Corral. It was between some cowboys and some lawmen.

The cowboys were two sets of brothers. They were Frank and Tom McLowry and Billy and Ike Clanton.

The lawmen were three brothers—Wyatt, Morgan, and Virgil Earp. The lawmen also had Doc Holliday, a famous gambler and gunfighter.

There had been a stagecoach robbery. The lawmen said that the cowboys were involved in the robbery. But some people in town felt that the lawmen had done it and were just trying to pin it on the cowboys.

Some people also thought that the cowboys were ready to leave town when they met near the O.K. Corral. The Earps and Doc Holliday came to the corral with their six-shooters at their sides. People lined the streets to watch. Guns blazed. Three of the cowboys were killed—Billy Clanton and Tom and Frank McLowry. Virgil and Morgan Earp were wounded.

The Earps were arrested for murder. But the judge let the Earps go.

Much of Arizona is still desert. You may think of a desert as a place where nothing grows. This is not true.

Cactus plants can live up to five years without rainfall. They store juice for times when there is no rain. Cacti

Giant
saguaro
cactus
plants

have lovely blossoms in the spring. And they bear fruit in
early summer.

The most famous cactus plants in Arizona are the
saguaros (sah • GAR • owes). They can live over 300 years.
They can grow over 50 feet tall. They are the largest
cactus plants in the United States. In May or June they
have pretty white flowers (the Arizona state flower). In
June or July the red fruits ripen.

Visit Saguaro National Monument near Tucson. It is a
desert area. You can see giant saguaro cactus plants.
And you can see many other kinds of cacti.

Prickly pear cactus

Other cacti that grow in Arizona include the organ-pipe, barrel cactus, Queen of the Night, and prickly pear.

The desert has a number of other unusual plants. The ocotillo (OKA • tee • yo) looks like some huge underwater plant. The desert willow has lovely pink flowers. The Joshua (JOSH • u • ah) tree (a kind of yucca) has a weird shape and lives to be very old. There are also many lovely wild flowers.

Mountain lions and bobcats live in Arizona's forests. Other Arizona animals include mountain sheep, black bears, foxes, elk, antelope, and deer. The pack rat likes to steal things. But it leaves you something — a pine cone or a piece of cactus — in return.

A pack rat

You can find rattlesnakes in Arizona. Road runners, birds that live in Arizona, can attack and eat young rattlesnakes. Scorpions (SCORE • pee • ens) live in the deserts. They sting with their tails and can have more than six eyes. Tarantulas (teh • RAN • cheh • lahs) — the biggest of all spiders — also live in the deserts. Tarantulas are big and hairy. They can grow up to six inches across in size. The bite of Arizona tarantulas is not very harmful, though.

There are 37 kinds of lizards that live in Arizona deserts. One is called the Gila monster. Its bite *is* poisonous.

There are still many ranches in Arizona today. Cowboys take care of cattle and sheepmen care for sheep on these ranches.

A re-creation of Coronado's journey into Arizona, at Coronado.

National Monument near Bisbee

Over 18 percent of all Arizonans are Mexican Americans (Americans of Mexican ancestry). Many Mexican Americans live in the southern part of the state, close to Mexico. Many live in Spanish-speaking neighborhoods, called *barrios*. In some Arizona schools, children are taught Spanish as well as English.

Throughout Arizona, you can see the influence of Mexican culture. You can see it in buildings. You can taste it in Mexican foods. There are also colorful Mexican-American festivals. *Fiestas* celebrating Mexican independence are held in Phoenix and Nogales.

Almost 100,000 Indians live in Arizona. Only Oklahoma has more Indians living there. But the Indians in Oklahoma were driven there from other places. Many of Arizona's tribes have lived there for hundreds of years.

A Navajo sheep herder

Many Indians live on reservations. There are 19 reservations in Arizona.

Like other groups, some Indians in Arizona follow the traditions and life-styles of long ago. Others have adopted more modern life-styles.

The Navajo are the biggest tribe in Arizona. Navajo Indians are famous for weaving rugs and blankets. Although these are beautiful, don't think that this is all the Navajo do. Some Navajo Indians are businessmen. Others raise sheep or cattle.

Many Apache Indians also raise cattle. The Havasupai Indians still live at the bottom of the Grand Canyon.

Lake Powell

Tonto National Monument

One interesting town on the Hopi Indian land is called
Oraibi (o • RI • bee). The Hopi Indians have lived in this
village for over 800 years. Many scientists think it is the
oldest town in the United States where people still live.

Home to Cliff Dwellers ... Basket Makers ...
Apache and Navajo Indians ... and now thousands of
retired people.

The land of Gila monsters ... tarantulas ... and the
towering saguaro cactus.

Famous for the Gunfight at the O.K. Corral ...
Geronimo's Indian wars ... and lost gold mines.

Natural wonders of the Painted Desert ... the Grand
Canyon ... and the Petrified Forest.

This is the Grand Canyon State—Arizona.

Facts About ARIZONA

Area—113,909 square miles (6th biggest state)

Greatest Distance North to South—395 miles

Greatest Distance East to West—340 miles

Borders—Utah on the north; New Mexico on the east; Mexico on the south; Nevada and California on the west

Highest Point—12,633 feet above sea level (Humphreys Peak)

Lowest Point—70 feet above sea level (in Yuma County, along the Colorado River)

Hottest Recorded Temperature—127° (at Parker, on July 7, 1905)

Coldest Recorded Temperature—Minus 40° (at Hawley Lake, on January 7, 1971)

Statehood—Our 48th state, on February 14, 1912

Origin of Name Arizona—From the Pima or Papago Indian word *Arizonac* (probably meaning "little spring")

Capital—Phoenix

Counties—14

U.S. Senators—2

U.S. Representatives—4

Electoral Votes—6

State Senators—30

State Representatives—60

43

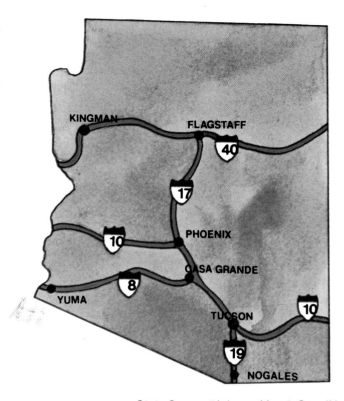

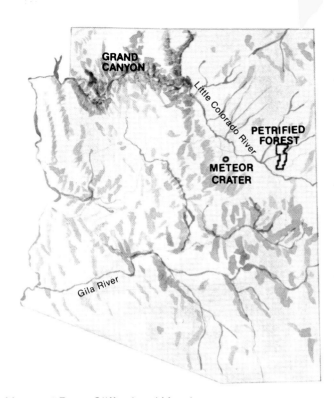

State Song—"Arizona March Song" by Margaret Rowe Clifford and Maurice Blumenthal

State Motto—*Ditat Deus* (Latin for "God Enriches")

Nicknames—The Grand Canyon State, the Copper State, Rattlesnake Heaven, Apache Hell, the Baby State, the Valentine State

State Seal—Adopted in 1910

State Flag—Adopted in 1917

State Flower—The flower of the saguaro cactus

State Bird—Cactus wren

State Tree—Palo verde

State Colors—Blue and old gold

Some Colleges and Universities—University of Arizona, Arizona State University, Grand Canyon College, Northern Arizona University, Navajo Community College

Principal Rivers—Colorado, Little Colorado, Gila, Bill Williams, Salt

Some Waterfalls—Bridal Veil, Beaver, Navajo, Havasu, Mooney

Animals—White-tail deer, mule deer, bighorn sheep, elk, mountain sheep, pronghorn antelope, badgers, beavers, foxes, javelinas (wild pigs), coyotes, bobcats, mountain lions, ocelots, black bears, rattlesnakes, coral snakes, king snakes, bull snakes, Arizona mud turtles, Gila monsters, scorpions, tarantulas, quails, road runners, trout, bass

Ranch and Farm Products—Cotton, beef cattle, lettuce, milk

Mining—Copper, gold, silver, zinc, petroleum, uranium

Manufacturing Products—Machinery, food products, glass products

Population—2,224,000 (1975 estimate)

44

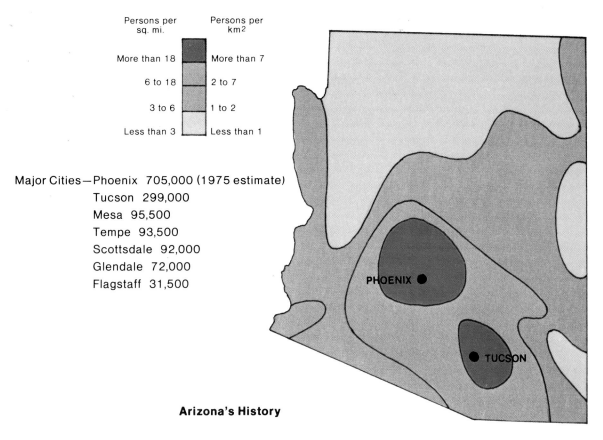

Persons per sq. mi.	Persons per km2
More than 18	More than 7
6 to 18	2 to 7
3 to 6	1 to 2
Less than 3	Less than 1

Major Cities—Phoenix 705,000 (1975 estimate)
  Tucson 299,000
  Mesa 95,500
  Tempe 93,500
  Scottsdale 92,000
  Glendale 72,000
  Flagstaff 31,500

Arizona's History

People came to live in Arizona at least 20,000 years ago. Some of the early people in Arizona are now known as the Cochise Man, Basket Makers, Pueblo people, Cliff Dwellers, and Hohokam (Canal Builders).

1200 A.D.—About this time the Hopi village of Oraibi, which may be the oldest American town where people have continuously lived, is founded
1539—Father Marcos de Niza, looking for cities of gold, explores Arizona and claims it for Spain
1540—Spanish explorer Coronado, also looking for gold, explores Arizona
1540—De Cardenas discovers Grand Canyon
Early 1600s—Spanish priests build churches
1680—In August, the Hopi Indians kill Spanish priests and burn missions
1692—Father Kino starts work and founds Guevavi mission
1700—San Xavier del Bac mission (White Dove of the Desert) is founded
1752—A presidio (fort) is built at Tubac in Santa Cruz Valley
1776—A presidio is built at Tucson
1821—Arizona now governed by Mexico
1848—At end of Mexican War most of Arizona becomes part of United States
1853—By Gadsden Purchase rest of Arizona becomes part of United States
1854—Copper is discovered in Arizona
1857—First stagecoach in Arizona
1858—Gold is discovered on Gila River

45

1862—Chief Cochise and Apaches attack soldiers at Apache Pass; Cochise battles white settlers for over ten years

1863—Territory of Arizona is created by United States Congress

1864—Kit Carson captures about 7,000 Navajo Indians in Canyon de Chelly; they are forced to leave Arizona

1864—Henry Wickenburg's burro helps him discover the Vulture Mine

1868—Settlement is made near present Phoenix

1869—John Wesley Powell explores the Grand Canyon by boat

1870—Population is 9,658

1881—Railroad crosses state

1881—The Gunfight at the O.K. Corral, on October 26

1886—The great Apache Chief Geronimo surrenders to U.S. soldiers on September 4; Indian fighting in Arizona is over

1889—Phoenix becomes the capital of the Arizona Territory

1890—Population is 88,243

1900—Population is 122,931

1911—Roosevelt Dam is completed

1912—On February 12 Arizona becomes the 48th state; the capital is Phoenix and George W.P. Hunt is the first governor

1919—Grand Canyon National Park is founded

1930—Coolidge Dam is completed

1930—The planet Pluto is discovered by Clyde Tombaugh at Lowell Observatory in Flagstaff

1936—Hoover Dam is completed

1940—Population of the Grand Canyon State is 499,261

1948—Indians obtain the right to vote

1949—Uranium is discovered on Navajo Reservation

1950—Population of growing state is 749,587

1960—Population has zoomed to 1,302,161

1963—United States Supreme Court decision maintains Arizona's right to large amount of Colorado River water

1964—Glen Canyon Dam is completed

1964—Barry M. Goldwater of Arizona runs for president but loses

1965—Judge Lorna Lockwood is elected chief justice of the Arizona Supreme Court; she is first woman in the U.S. to govern a state supreme court

1967—In December, a blizzard hits Arizona with seven feet of snow

1968—London Bridge, which was falling down, is moved to Arizona

1968—United States Congress authorizes Central Arizona Project to bring waters of Colorado River to Phoenix and Tucson

1969—Navajo Community College is built at Many Farms; moves to Tsaile in 1973

1978—Bruce Babbitt is elected governor in November

1978—Floods hit Arizona

INDEX

47

INDEX, Cont'd.

About the Author:

Dennis Fradin attended Northwestern University on a creative writing scholarship and graduated in 1967. While still at Northwestern, he published his first stories in *Ingenue* magazine and also won a prize in *Seventeen's* short story competition. A prolific writer, Dennis Fradin has been regularly publishing stories in such diverse places as *The Saturday Evening Post, Scholastic, National Humane Review, Midwest,* and *The Teaching Paper.* He has also scripted several educational films. Since 1970 he has taught second grade reading in a Chicago school—a rewarding job, which, the author says, "provides a captive audience on whom I test my children's stories." Married and the father of three children, Dennis Fradin spends his free time with his family or playing a myriad of sports and games with his childhood chums.

About the Artists:

Len Meents studied painting and drawing at Southern Illinois University and after graduation in 1969 he moved to Chicago. Mr. Meents works full time as a painter and illustrator. He and his wife and child currently make their home in LaGrange, Illinois.

Richard Wahl, graduate of the Art Center College of Design in Los Angeles, has illustrated a number of magazine articles and booklets. He is a skilled artist and photographer who advocates realistic interpretations of his subjects. He lives with his wife and two sons in Libertyville, Illinois.